MY DOG AND ME

Written by Tracy Voss

Illustrated by Marcy Tippmann

Dedication

My sweet Milton,

You have been one of my favorite rescues to date. You taught me that life can be so unfair to those of us with good hearts. But through hard times, we learn to recognize and appreciate the good things in life. You ran, hid, and dodged some of the best rescuers in San Antonio for years. After you were caught, I realized you ran to protect yourself from more heartache. But somehow, you were able to see the goodness in my heart from the first time we met. You looked at me as if I was your long lost friend. The truth is. . . I was. Watching and helping you heal was one of the most rewarding experiences of my life. Once broken and not trusting of anyone, you blossomed into a loving dog that everyone adores. You left your hardships behind you and moved on to live your best life with a wonderful family.

You are the definition of Live Like a Dog *and I love you, Milton.*

My Dog and Me
©2023 Tracy Voss
All rights reserved.

979-8-9864244-3-9 – Hardcover
979-8-9864244-4-6 – Softcover
979-8-9864244-5-3 – Ebook
979-8-9864244-6-0 – Spanish Edition

First edition 2023
Printed in the United States of America
Live Like a Dog, LLC
PO Box 849
Hondo, TX 78861
LiveLikeaDog.press

Book Designer: Marcy Tippmann
Project Manager: Andrea Leigh Ptak

My name is Adalyn.

I am 11 years old.

When I was 6, I got my very own puppy. Her name is Dixie and she's a rescue from Texas. She was born under a porch at a tire shop. I loved her from the moment I first saw her. She is my best friend.

Do you have a best friend?

I was very sick when I first got Dixie. I had an operation on my heart and had to stay home from school to rest and get better. But instead of getting better, I got sick again. My parents took me to the doctor and we found out I had leukemia, which is a kind of cancer. But please don't be sad for me, I am okay now.

When I had cancer, things were really hard for me. But Dixie stayed right by my side and even slept in my bed with me at night. She always knew when I wasn't feeling good and she would give me kisses.

On days when I felt better, we played games and she would chase me around the house. We had so much fun. Dogs are almost always happy, and when I am with Dixie she helps me be happy too.

I had go to the hospital a lot and had to leave Dixie at home. I showed all the doctors and nurses pictures of her and talked about her all the time. I didn't want to stay there overnight because Dixie needed me to help take care of her. Dogs need people to give them love, water, food, and a nice place to sleep.

When I would get back home, guess who was always waiting for me? Dixie! Her tail was always wagging and her butt was always wiggling.

Can you wiggle your butt like my dog Dixie?

I've had Dixie for 5 years now and we are still best friends. I don't have cancer anymore and we get to play every day. She helped me get better and I will always love her.

I wish kids never got sick and no one had cancer. . . and everyone had a dog.

A dog will always be your best friend. When you don't feel good, your dog will always stay with you. They love us no matter what.

Hi, my name is Letty.

I am 10 years old.

I have a dog named Bear. I named her this because she looks like a black bear. She is my best friend.

On most days, I don't want to go to school because the other kids don't like me and they tease me behind my back. No one wants to play with me. They call me names and make fun of the way I look and what I wear.

When the bus driver stops in front of my house, I can hear the kids laughing. My house doesn't look like their houses. It is messy and has lots of junk in the front yard. Sometimes my mom and dad are fighting when I get off the school bus and the other kids can hear them.

It's not nice to tease people. When I get teased it hurts my feelings. That's another reason I love my dog Bear so much, she never teases me.

Does anyone ever tease you?

Bear has to stay outside in the backyard. She waits for me every day to come home. My parents won't let her come inside because they say she's dirty and full of bugs. They say dogs don't belong inside. When I grow up, I am going to let her in my house with me.

I never feel alone or different when Bear is with me. She doesn't care that I wear old clothes or that I look messy sometimes. She always wags her tail when she sees me and gives me kisses. She loves me just the way I am.

Bear stays right by my side and watches over me when we go places together. She likes to chase me around and when she catches me, I roll around on the ground with her and it makes me laugh.

When I have a bad day at school, I come home and cry into her fur and hug her neck. She always licks the tears from my cheeks and it tickles. When we are together, I don't think about school, things at home, or anything that makes me sad. I think about how much I love her and how much she loves me.

I bring her food and always make sure she has clean water. When it's cold outside, I put blankets in her doghouse.

When you have a dog, you always have someone who loves you. I am never alone when I am with Bear.

Hi, my name is Miguel.

I am almost 9 years old but I don't look it. I am smaller than the other boys in my grade. I am not good at sports and the other boys never want me on their teams. They call me names and tell me I should go play with the girls and that I look like a baby.

My dad doesn't live with us anymore and my mom doesn't have time to teach me how to play sports. So instead, I play with my dog, Zoomba. She is a little, white dog that my mom found on the streets when it was really cold outside.

Zoomba cuddles with me and sleeps on
my bed. When I get home from school, she is
so excited to see me.

At school yesterday, I tried to join the other boys playing baseball. But they wouldn't let me play with them because I wasn't good enough. So I took out the picture of Zoomba I carry in my backpack and told her I would be home soon to play ball with her. It made me feel better.

We play ball every single day. I throw it for her and she brings it back. Zoomba never laughs at me if I have a bad throw. I try to throw it farther and farther each day. I am getting better and better, and one day, I hope I am so good I can be on a little league baseball team.

I love my dog so much. I never feel alone because of Zoomba and she never makes fun of me when I make mistakes. She is my best friend.

Then one day, something magical happened at school.

Do you remember Adalyn, the girl with a dog named Dixie? At recess, Adalyn didn't feel well enough to play with the other kids. She saw me sitting alone so she walked over and asked me if I wanted to see a picture of her dog, Dixie. Just like me, she brings it to school every day!

Adalyn was so nice to me and she was so excited to see my picture of Zoomba! We talked and talked about our dogs.

While we were talking, Adalyn spotted Letty crying near the soccer field. We knew the other kids teased her. Adalyn said we could cheer her up by showing her pictures of our dogs. What we didn't know was that Letty has a dog too! Her name is Bear, and Letty had a picture of her in her backpack. She had the biggest smile on her face when she showed us her dog.

And for the rest of recess, time stood still and we laughed and laughed. Adalyn didn't feel sick anymore, I didn't care that the other boys didn't let me play ball with them, and Letty didn't think about being teased.

After school, we met at the dog
park with our dogs so they could
play. It was the best day ever!

Even though we are all different,
we became best friends that day
because of our love for our dogs.

Never forget to *Live Like a Dog*. . . It is the secret to being happy. Dogs don't care if you're rich or poor, sick or healthy, or if you're like all the other kids. . . they just love you the way you are. We should be more like dogs with each other.

Hi, it's Adalyn again. After meeting Miguel and Letty, I learned that dogs help people in so many different ways.

Service/Assistance Dogs

You might already know about guide dogs for blind people, but did you know that dogs help people with all kinds of special needs? Some dogs alert people who have hearing loss to doorbells and other sounds. They can carry or fetch things for people who use wheelchairs or walkers. Or, they can provide emotional support for people with autism and act as a way to help them make friends. They can sniff out life-threatening allergens like peanuts and sound a warning so their human doesn't eat them accidentally. They can even be trained to alert their human companions to dangerous medical conditions like diabetes, seizures, and heart attacks. All of these dogs are so much more than just companions—they are often lifesavers and help their humans lead more normal lives.

Therapy Dogs

These dogs are people's pets who get special training to do important volunteer work along with their human companions. Any dog with a friendly, outgoing personality has the makings of a therapy dog. Dog and human teams visit places where people can benefit from the special kind of love a dog can give. They give seniors in nursing homes time with a furry friend, encourage physical therapy patients to do their exercises, and help children in hospitals feel less anxious. They can also act as an uncritical listener for beginner readers in schools and libraries, soothe the nerves of college students during exam week, and comfort survivors of disasters. There are several programs that offer training around the country, but the first was *Pet Partners,* which allows kids as young as 10 to train through their online course.

Search & Rescue Dogs

You might have seen these dogs on television sniffing in the rubble of a building after an earthquake or searching in the woods for a lost person. But did you know that they are usually just pets and their owners who have taken years of training so they could help others? The dogs need to be very athletic, so certain breeds do better than others: German Shepherds, Labradors, Golden Retrievers, and Border Collies tend to make good search and rescue dogs. They search for missing people in all kinds of places from big cities to wilderness areas. Using their tracking skills, they help find survivors after disasters or hikers lost in the mountains by sniffing the ground and air. These

teams make a big commitment to do this job and need to be able to act when the need arises. It's not for everyone but very rewarding for those who take it on.

Just like Dixie, Bear, and Zoomba, all of these dogs are also pets to the people they share their lives with. They love their people and cuddle and play just like any other dog, but they also have a special job to do too! A dog is the best friend anyone can have.

PAWS, Promoting Animal Welfare in Schools, is an educational program for elementary school children that encourages compassion for all living creatures.

Tracy Voss has been rescuing dogs since she was a little girl. She has been associated with non-profit dog rescue since 2010 and currently volunteers all of her spare time with Tracy's Paws Rescue which she founded with Rhonda Harmon in 2020.

Live Like a Dog PAWS teaches children through educational books and hands-on learning activities how to become ambassadors for responsible pet ownership and kindness to all living creatures—including people.

Live Like a Dog PAWS develops and strengthens the human–animal bond, which can be a source of comfort for many children who have difficulties at home or at school.

All young children need support and guidance to have healthy relationships within their immediate families and friends. This includes relationships with their pets. For many kids, their pets are their best friends. For some children, their pets might provide the only stable relationship and unconditional love they experience while they are growing up.

Strengthening the human-animal bond can improve self-esteem and give children a sense of purpose as well as encouraging them to show compassion towards all living creatures. This program will provide the children with some helpful tools they can use to lead happy lives despite the many challenges they may face in their life.

It is our belief that every child desires to provide their pets with the same quality of care they deserve and want themselves. All children want a loving, healthy, and safe environment to grow up in. Helping children be a part of their own pet's care or allowing them to play a role in helping unwanted pets teaches responsibility and accountability in all aspects of life.

Live Like a Dog

Live Like a Dog LLC is an educational company founded by Tracy Voss in 2021. It promotes compassion for all living creatures by publishing books about real rescue dogs and educating children through the PAWS program.

Crusty and His Red Sweater

The Amazing Story of a Real-Life Rescue Dog

This is the true story of how one dog was saved from a life on the streets near the border of Mexico, brought back to health with love and care, and found the perfect home 1,200 miles away from where he started.

Meet Edward

The Real-Life Ambassador for PAWS

This is the true story of Edward, a dog who didn't let his physical differences keep him from making friends. After months of waiting, Edward finally finds his forever home and his new role— helping elementary school children learn about animal welfare.

Dixie has the ickies

The Amazing Story of a Real-Life Rescue Dog

Little Dixie was born under a porch at a tire shop, where her mom and siblings had too little food and too many bugs. Her luck changed when she and her family were rescued and she found a home with a very special purpose.

www.ingramcontent.com/pod-product-compliance
Lightning Source LLC
Chambersburg PA
CBHW041528120626
46551CB00018B/2616